A Choice Theory Psychology Guide to

ADDICTIONS

Ways To Overcome Substance Dependence
And Other Compulsive Behaviors

I0421920

Michael Rice

From The "Choice Theory in Action" Series

ISBN: 9781070689302

CONTENTS

The Choice Theory In Action Series

This is one of a series of short books aimed at helping people gain better control of their lives using ideas from Choice Theory psychology, a theory of human behaviour that was developed by Reality Therapy creator Dr. William Glasser.

In this selection of books we explain the application of Choice Theory psychology to a range of popular themes such as   Addiction, Anger, Depression, Happiness, Parenting, Relationships, and Stress. The authors are all experts in Choice Theory psychology and all have studied directly under its creator, Dr. William Glasser.

Mike Rice has worked as a licensed therapist specializing in drug and alcohol abuse and has written several books on the application of Choice Theory psychology to this area.   In this book his aim is to give you some understanding of the why and how of addictive behaviors and what can be done to acquire the power to control them with Choice Theory applications.

Brian Lennon
Series Editor

Acknowledgments

I am extremely grateful for all of my fellow Choice Theory certified members, especially Senior Faculty Member Bob Hoglund; the late Wm Glasser Institute Administrator Linda Harshman; Senior Faculty Member Georgie Hofhine; the current U.S. and International Administrator of Wm Glasser Institute, Kim Daub-Olver; Senior Faculty Member Ivan Honey of Australia who was my certification instructor; my book editor Lynn Zacny Busby; and all the many members of the Institute throughout the United States and other countries whom I have met though our National and International conferences.

A final offer of deepest gratitude goes to my best friend and Choice Theory advocate, the late Dr. Ken Larsen. Ken was very supportive and instrumental in the writing of my books and my workshop presentations as well as for our Internet friendship that endured for only a short time, across the many miles that separated us.

Mike Rice

Preface

Many books and applications for treating addiction have been created over the years and, for the most part, all tend to contain some valuable and effective information and directives. Primarily, their focus is on getting the client clean and sober, and, hopefully, maintaining abstinence. What is missing in the majority of these programs is the identification and focus of the underlying cause of one's unhappiness that led to their internalized and biochemically affected addiction. Without this identification and focus, the underlying problem that eventually led to compulsive use will always be a threat for relapse.

Relying on alcohol/drug/compulsive behaviors are ways to avoid having to face and endure unhappiness. When life hands us disappointments, frustration, conflicts in relationships followed by feeling powerless to deal with it all, the most common behavior is to find those things that provide pleasure and distract the unhappiness. This is how addictions and compulsive behaviors begin. Aside from natural disasters, poverty, and war, the primary cause of unhappiness is the result of unsatisfying relationships with the important people in a person's life or having no relationships at all.

Even when an intervention is conducted, the interventionist calls upon all of the client's important people in their life. However, I don't agree with the methods utilized in many of these interventions as they tend to blindside the client as well as criticize, blame, complain, nag, punish, threaten and even bribe the client to stop their behavior. More times than not, the client will defiantly resist going into treatment because they feel ganged up on and being forced to do something that is not of their liking or of their own decision.

The Choice Theory approach does not rely on external controlling methods but rather, discovering what the client really would want his or her life to be; identifying the important people in their life; evaluating the client's choices and how their methods either helped or harmed their relationships; allowing clients the freedom and respect to make their own decisions on how to improve their life; and creating a plan on how to get what they want in their lives.

People are more inclined to improve their life when it is their own idea, feel respected, and don't feel threatened or coerced to do something they don't want to do.

"The most profound personal growth doesn't happen when reading a book or meditating on a mat. It happens in the throes of conflict . . . when you are angry, afraid, frustrated. It happens when you are doing the same old thing and you suddenly realize you have a choice." Veronica Tugaleva

My intention in this book is to give you information explaining what motivates you and why you behave the way you do. The only thing we receive from the world outside ourselves is information.

Information, alone, does not make us do what we do. We always have choices on how we react to external or outside information. Understanding and learning about the difference between a failing external control psychiatry and effective internal control psychiatry will be the key to discovering ways to take responsibility to help you overcome addiction and take charge of your life.

Not only have thousands of clients been my teacher, but Dr. Glasser's Choice Theory has resulted in incredible results with my clients and a powerful affect on my personal life. While this book is directed to those with compulsive behaviors, Choice Theory is a relatively new psychology that serves all long term emotional and maladaptive behaviors such as anxiety, depression, bipolar, schizophrenia, personality disorders, PTSD, Domestic Violence, Relationship problems, and many other behaviors that are causing people problems and unhappiness in their lives.

You may notice text that is repeated several times throughout this book for a reason: It often takes reading and hearing important points several times before "sinking in." I thought I knew all about Choice Theory after reading it one time. I learned so much more each time I read it. Reading and hearing something at least three times tend to leave a lasting impression.

It is through the experiences of my clients, Dr. Glasser's work and creation of Choice Theory, and the honor of being asked to contribute to the Choice Theory In Action Series books created by Brian Lennon, that I am able to share this knowledge with you, the reader.

1. Can You Recognize An Addiction?

Alcohol has been in use for thousands of years. Beer has been found to be buried in the pyramids of Egypt as well as pay stubs of 5,000 years ago for wages paid with beer for the pyramid builders. So, you would think that after more than five thousand years, all that can be known about alcohol should be known by now. Yet today, there are more myths, lies, and half-truths pertaining to alcoholism addiction. Just what is an addiction?

The Merriam Webster Dictionary defines addiction as the following:
The compulsive need for and use of a habit-forming substance (such as heroin, nicotine, or alcohol) characterized by tolerance and by well-defined physiological symptoms upon withdrawal; broadly defined: Addiction is a persistent compulsive use of a substance or compulsive behavior known by the user to be harmful.

This is very simple definition of a complex condition that omits the effects it has on the individual and those close to them.

I define an addiction as a compulsive behavior that eases frustration and stress of unwanted emotions or situations. It has the effect of sedating the brain either by mood altering substances or behaviors that relieve stress and unhappiness. The addictive behavior, while affording pleasure, distracts from one's unhappiness, and causes problems for the individual as well as the important people in his or her life. The behavior is continued regardless of the problems it causes. It is further characterized by withdrawal symptoms either emotionally, physically, or both upon any period of deprivation or cessation. Any attempt to stop will cause withdrawal reactions that lead to anxiety, fear, nausea, diarrhea, sweating, irritability, trouble concentrating, headaches, hallucinations, and even seizures or death.

Drugs And Alcohol Are Not The Only Addictions You May Have

The compulsive behaviors of gambling, sex, gaming, indiscriminate spending, workaholics, and other compulsive behaviors tend to have withdrawal symptoms of anxiety, restlessness, poor concentration, and irritability but not necessarily life-threatening symptoms more commonly associated with substance addictions.

Non-substance addictive behaviors are those that involve inordinate amounts of time that tend to distance one's self from spouses, family, and friends. There are some people who may refer to some of these behaviors as "Positive Addictions" because they aren't drug or alcohol affected behaviors. However, if they interfere with the needs of others and cause relationship problems, they are not "Positive" at all.

Non-substance addictive behaviors are associated more with boredom, powerlessness, and/or the need to satisfy one's Power Needs of competing, achieving, succeeding, and winning. The genetic reward for obsessive gaming is the excitement of winning and accomplishment. It often gives the person an elevated sense of self-worth. Whatever the motivation behind these addictions, they will be rooted in unsatisfying relationship issues with others, or no relationships at all, and/or a means of escape to avoid having to face their unhappiness or take measures to improve them.

Dr. Peter Breggin states that obsessions and compulsions focus attention on persistent thoughts or ritualized activities rather than on the overwhelming emotions of frustration, shame and guilt, anxiety, and unhappiness in one's life.[i]

Do You Have An Addiction?

Addiction behaviors ultimately result in the loss of friends, jobs, marriages, families, and lives. The problems they cause are therefore the symptoms of addiction. When assessing substance addiction, a very simple question to ask yourself is, "Do normal drinkers behave like this?"

The following list is just some of the problems and behaviors associated with addictive behavior. Identifying any two or more of them suggests you take a closer look at your use or behavior.

1. Drinking more than intended. (loss of control)

2. Not recalling things said and done after a time of drinking/using.

3. Hiding the behavior from others.

---

i   Breggin, Peter, MD, Toxic Psychiatry, p. 232, St. Martin's Press, NY, 1991

4. Harmed relationships.

5. Family and friend concerns.

6. Drinking alone so that others won't notice how often or how much is consumed.

7. Lying about drinking/using.

8. Stealing or selling items for money to buy drugs or alcohol.

9. Missing work/school or drinking on the job.

10. Passing out.

11. Drinking or using to overcome withdrawal symptoms when trying to quit.

12. Spouse or significant other threatens to leave, or actually does leave, if the behavior is not stopped.

13. Loss of employment due to missed work or showing up late.

14. Physical complications of the liver, pancreas, heart, esophagus, stomach, lungs, neurological problems, or intestines.

15. Advised by a doctor to stop drinking/using but continuing to do so anyway.

16. Getting into fights or arguments that only seem to happen when drinking/using.

17. Buying drugs and/or alcohol when one cannot really afford the expense.

18. Spending hours on video games or porn sites while foregoing responsibilities.

19. Compulsive gambling in casinos or other venues while owing money or not paying household bills and family obligations.

20. Indiscriminate sex or spending time thinking or performing sex with or without partners.

21. Choosing repetitive behaviors to avoid facing current problems and unwanted emotions.

22. Defiant denial that a problem exists when others can clearly recognize it.

23. DUI arrests.

24. Drinking 15 or more drinks a week.

25. Drinking 4 or more drinks in an hour.

How Did I Become Addicted?

Simply stated, substance addiction is the result of the continued use of an addictive substance that the body and brain have become accustomed to and rely upon in order to feel good. If drugs and alcohol didn't make you feel good, you couldn't give them away. They offer a sense of euphoria and distract your unhappiness.

Non-substance addictive behaviors are somewhat different. Those behaviors are relied upon to bring pleasure, excitement, and the thrill of winning or achieving something while, at the same time, making the days and hours of unhappiness or boredom seem shorter. Primarily, they function to avoid having to take responsibility for improving one's situation because they don't want to do something that is necessary to improve their situation, or they don't know how to do what is necessary to improve their situation. In other words: To escape from stress and anxiety and replace their general unhappiness with pleasure.

"I Heard It's Genetic."

No gene has ever been identified to date to substantiate that claim. Several articles have been written by those who claim they have found a link or a genetic marker that "might," "could," "suggests," that addictions are genetic but they disappear as quickly as they were announced. Those who report the genetic association and those who research and study while seeking a genetic connection start by observing any family history of addiction.

"Well, his father was an alcoholic so it must be genetic."

"Both his father and his grandfather were alcoholics so this proves it's genetic. It runs in the family."

Both of the above statements are faulty deductive assumptions without regard to the identification of any specific gene to addictions or even other mental health issues. So, if it's not genetic, what is it?

Do people who live in different geological locations speak with different accents of their common language because of genetics? Where did you learn how to put on a pillow case, iron a shirt, prepare a specific recipe, or any other task or behavior? It is learned behavior from observation of others or self-discovered behavior.

When a newlywed husband noticed his wife cutting off the end of a roast before putting it in the oven , he asked her why she did that. She told him that her mother always did that. When he asked his mother-in-law why she cut off the end of the roast, she replied, "Because that's how MY mother always did it." The husband eventually found himself in the company of his wife's grandmother so he took the opportunity to ask her why she would cut the end of the roast off before putting it in the oven. The grandmother replied, "Because I never had a pan large enough for it to fit in." The behavior is far from being genetic.

Family line substance abuse addictions are the result of learned behavior by observation as well as a self-discovered means to deal with unhappiness. If you observed a parent or other relative who routinely relied on substance abuse to deal with their stress and unhappiness, you have a high probability of relying on the behavior to deal with your own stress and unhappiness.

My explanation is a simple one which tends to be viewed as too simple and naive for many to accept. They consider addictions and behaviors to be more complex and of a physical or medical cause. When challenged that no medical or genetic identification has been discovered to prove or make a genetic connection, the standard common response is: "It's in there. We just haven't found it yet." Then society continues to believe the myth and scientists continue to seek something that isn't there.

Pleasure vs Happiness

In both cases of substance and non-substance addictions, there is an intense feeling of pleasure that is mistakenly considered to be happiness. There is a distinct difference between Pleasure and Happiness and how they are attained. Pleasure is short-lived. Therefore, the behavior that causes pleasure must be repeated often in order to maintain it. Happiness is much less intense than pleasure but it lasts much longer than pleasure. Pleasure can be attained without the need of another person to be involved in the behavior. Happiness, however, can only be attained by having meaningful relationships with the important people in your life.

One of my past careers was that of a traveling musician/entertainer with a six-member act. We traveled all over the United States and got paid to do so. I preferred to travel alone as we lived, rehearsed, and worked together all the days we weren't traveling. Traveling alone offered me solitude and time to enjoy my own company. While I would enjoy these moments, there were often times that made them not so enjoyable.

Traveling as much as we did, I got to see parts of our country that I never knew existed. I would stop my car to take in the view and suddenly find myself feeling sad instead of happy. The problem was . . . I had no one to share the experience with me. Dr. Glasser said, "Imagine you are a golfer and playing a round of golf by yourself. On the first par three hole, you sink a hole-in-one. How excited will you be if you are the only one to have seen and experience it?" Had others been with you, your happiness would have lasted longer and been more enjoyable. Happiness is therefore the result of having meaningful relationships in your life. The more meaningful relationships you have, the happier you will be.

External Control

External Control is what so many people rely on when they want others to behave the way they

want them to behave.   When we first meet
someone we like, we tend to overlook the things
we don't like about them.   When the honeymoon
stage of the relationship begins to wane, you
attempt to get your partner to stop or change
behaviors that you chose to overlook early in your
relationship. You no longer choose to ignore them.
Unhappiness will result when either you or your
partner begin to attempt to control each other. You
overlooked it before because you *chose* to do so.

1. *You wanted someone else to do what he or she*
   refused to do. Usually in a variety of ways, some
   blatant, some devious, you were trying to force
   him or her to do what you wanted.
2. *Someone else was trying to make you to do*
   something you didn't want to do.
3. *Both of you or someone else were trying to make*
   each other do what neither wanted to do.
4. *You were trying to force yourself to do something*
   you found very painful or even impossible to do.ii

External Control is the behavior of trying to control
others to get them to do what you want them to
do. It relies on the faulty belief system that people
and events outside yourself "make" you behave
the way you do . . . that your unhappiness is the
result of what others do or don't do. You believe
that you can get others to do what you want them
to do and others can do the same with you. You
may even believe that you have the right to control
others by criticizing, blaming, complaining,
nagging, threatening, punishing, bribing, and
rewarding.

----

ii Glasser, Wm., "Choice Theory," pp. 13, 14, Harper Collins,
NY, 1998

These behaviors have never been successful and they do just the opposite of what is desired for the outcome. Instead of bringing each other closer together, they drive each other apart resulting in loss of respect and love. The nature of external control is that once it is used on someone, they will automatically use external control behaviors in retaliation and defense. As Dr. Glasser says, "External Control begets External Control."

By eliminating as many of the relationship destroying behaviors listed above, you can expect to experience an almost instantaneous happiness and contentment. Once you stop doing external control, others will begin to listen and respect you. They will not have the need to fight back or become defensive and argumentative. While they may continue to use external control on you, you always have a choice on how you will react to them. Remember . . . it takes two to fight. If facing an opponent in argumentative or combative ways, they will tire easily and not find it very rewarding if you are not fighting, resisting, or arguing with them.

I Need To Satisfy My Discomfort

Avoiding unhappiness is a natural behavior for anyone with common sense. If we don't want to get wet in the rain, we seek shelter, use an umbrella, or wear rain protective clothing. If cold, we put on a sweater or coat to keep warm. If hungry or thirsty, we seek food to feel satisfied and beverages to slake thirst. We take controlling measures to satisfy our unhappiness or unpleasant situations. It's when we begin to choose behaviors that are meant to control someone else, whom we perceive as the cause of our unhappiness, that we get into trouble.

Addictive behaviors are the most common forms of escape. At best, they are only temporary relief from one's unhappiness by anesthetizing the brain, giving a sense of euphoria and, at worst, causing relationship problems, emotional problems, financial problems, divorce, health problems, employment problems, and even death.

This Is How You Got There

The first time someone has a drink or uses a drug, they have an immediate experience both physically and emotionally. Some find pleasure in it while others may be turned off by it while they may possibly later return to it for its obvious effects. If not accustomed to the drug, the body may expel it by vomiting, feeling nauseous or coughing depending upon how the drug is being used. Others may merely feel pleasure as the substance reaches the pleasure/reward center of the brain in the limbic area known as the nucleus accumbens. The more one uses the substance, the more the body becomes accustomed to its presence. As tolerance increases, larger amounts of the drug are needed to maintain the wanted effect.

Inhibitions are lowered. A sense of euphoria is felt. Cares and woes tend to melt away while enjoying the pleasures of the drug. (Alcohol is a drug in liquid form). While blood alcohol levels continue to rise with each drink, the person may experience laughter and find things amusing. When blood alcohol levels begin to fall, things aren't so funny or amusing and depression sets in as certain unwanted emotions and situations return to mind with accompanying physical discomfort.

The first path to addiction is **Sociological abuse**. Very few people start out drinking alone. It is while in the company of others who are drinking that a sense of conviviality occurs. You all have something in common: Everyone is drinking or using and feeling similar physical and emotional drugged effects. A sense of camaraderie exists as you joke, laugh, flirt, and feel euphoric. You perceive this stage as "having fun" until you sober up and don't feel so very happy, have hangovers, and become dehydrated. Socializing becomes the primary cause for getting together to collectively enjoy the effects of drinking/using. This stage becomes a favorite way to have fun by getting together, laughing, and flirting with fewer inhibitions than when sober.

The second path to addiction is **Psychological abuse** and is developed alongside the sociological development of use. One quickly learns that when they drink or use, they experience the loss of stress and unwanted emotions they were experiencing before they began drinking/using/ or a compulsive behavior. Unhappy situations tend to melt away as long as they drink, use, or behave compulsively. They drink to "relax" after a long day at work or from a stressful or harrowing experience. We often hear others say, or even say ourselves, "Whew! I need a drink." The drug is used to deal with unhappy and uncomfortable situations and becomes routinely relied upon for future unpleasant situations in the form of self-medicating.

Those who drink alcohol learn relatively quickly how a few drinks can create a sense of apathy regarding unwanted issues or concerns albeit only temporary. Alcohol becomes a temporary solution while, at the same time, becoming a long-lasting problem.

The two stages of sociological and psychological abuse are very strong and difficult to overcome once established. If given up for any period of time, withdrawal symptoms of anxiety, depressing, and stressing often occur. As difficult as they are to overcome, they are still not as difficult to deal with the third path to addiction when one crosses the line into the third stage of **Bio-cellular addiction.**

The continued use of addictive substances causes the body and internal organs to work overtime in metabolizing the substance. To process just one drink takes the body one hour to metabolize. The liver must change it into four different components before it is eliminated. The first change the liver does is to turn it into an extremely toxic chemical called acetaldehyde. The acetaldehyde then circulates throughout the body's organs and cells and then the liver turns the acetaldehyde into acidic acid. After the acidic acid travels a third time throughout the body's organs and cells, the liver then turns the acidic acid into two more chemical changes: carbon dioxide and water, which are eliminated through your lungs when you breathe and by urination through the kidneys.

This process cannot be speeded up. In time, however, it can be slowed down due to damage to the liver. Liver cells die and the liver does not have the full capacity to metabolize the substance than it normally would if healthy.

The substance affects every cell of the body and brain. At first, the body does its best to eliminate it. The more the substance is used, the more the body's cells decide not to have to work so hard to get rid of it. The cells, which are not normally structured to function with the constant use of the substance, change their molecular structure in order to function with the drug's regular presence.

Once a person crosses the line to bio-cellular addiction, any period of deprivation or attempts to quit will cause the cells to have a negative reaction causing the person intense physical and emotional distress. This is why so many individuals relapse when they try to quit on their own. They felt better physically and emotionally when they were using than when they weren't. Incidentally, this also applies to prescription opiate meds, antidepressant, anxiety medications, and any other psychoactive medication. The addict/alcoholic and those who are addicted to other behaviors feel ill or out to sorts when not drinking/using or behaving compulsively. They feel better or even "normal" when drinking/using/behaving.

Tell someone who is addicted that they can get their life back by attending ninety days of inpatient treatment; the addict knows that he can feel better in twenty seconds or less. Which behavior do you think they would choose?

Anyone who attempts to stop drinking or using may experience severe physical withdrawal symptoms. If so, they should seek medical supervision to detoxify their body before continuing to stop.

Detox and continued abstinence will cause some cells to return to normal functioning but not all of them. Once the line to bio-cellular addiction has been crossed, there can be no turning back without awakening those remaining altered cells that expect and thrive on the presence of alcohol or drugs. This phenomenon does not exist with non-substance dependency but if the behavior is mentally recalled to bring relief from unpleasant situations and no newly formed healthy coping skills have been learned, one can easily return to compulsive use and behaviors. Abstinence is one component of overcoming addiction. Recovery is the learning of new and healthier coping skills. So, this is where we will begin . . . by taking control of your life and learning new life skills.

2. Why You Behave The Way You Do

From the moment you wake each morning 'til the moment you go to sleep, you are hard wired genetically to acquire five Basic Needs. These needs motivate you to do any and all the things that you do your entire life, all day long. All human beings on earth, regardless of race or culture have these genetic needs. The only difference is how they go about meeting them.

Your Five Basic Genetic Needs To Be Happy

Survival: Food, Shelter, Clothing, Transportation, Adequate Finances, Physical and Emotional Health, and Reproduction.

Love & Belonging: To give and receive love from the important people in your life and having a healthy group of friends and associates: The love of your parents, siblings, children, and significant other. Having a meaningful relationship with at least one person and preferably more than one is a sole element of happiness.

Power: The need to be appreciated, respected; to achieve; to compete, and to be recognized.

Freedom: The ability to come and go as you please; to make your own decisions and careers and choices of your own volition; Freedom from legal and financial problems; Having a valid driver's license; Possessing freedom from the throes of addiction and those who try to control you.

Fun: To recreate and share pleasurable times with meaningful relationships. To learn. The genetic reward for learning is fun. The school courses you took in which you excelled are those in which the teacher made it fun and/or you found them to be interesting and enjoyable.

There is nothing that you do that does not have any one or more of these Basic Needs as the source or impetus for all your behavior. Any unhappiness you experience will be due to the unmet needs of any one or more of these needs. Not everyone has the same value of your needs. Some have stronger or weaker needs than you may have.

I contend that when the need for Love and Belonging is met, the remaining needs are more easily attained. This makes Love and Belonging an important and major role in finding and maintaining happiness and the recovery process from addiction.

What's Missing In Your Life?

In the chart that follows, write the numbers from 1 to 5 in the "What I Need" column with 1 being the least important to you and 5 being the most important to you. Then in the next column, write the numbers from 0 to 5 of how satisfied you feel these individual needs are being met right now at this time in your life. You can repeat the same number value for the different wants and haves.

	What I Want & Need	What I Have
Survival		
Love & Belonging		
Power		
Freedom		
Fun		

A difference of 3 or more indicate those areas of your life that are missing or need to be improved towards attaining happiness. For example: If the value you give for Love and Belonging is 4 and you feel that you only have it a rating of 1 or 0, you have just identified a major cause of your unhappiness. If you have a history of long-term substance abuse, it would not be unusual for all five areas of your Basic Needs to be lacking and requiring improvement.

Any Basic Need that has a ratings difference of 2 or more indicate what is lacking in your life and what needs to be addressed in order to find the happiness and peace of mind that you want to have. The wider the distance between the rating of what you need and what you have identifies how serious the concern for improvement and the severity of your unhappiness.

How Addictions Affect Your Basic Needs

Survival

If addicted, you are relying on your drug of choice, or some other compulsive behavior, as a means of Survival . . . to get through the day and not feel tense, nervous, anxious, sick, and any other unwanted emotions. The need for your drug or drink can be so severe that you may even consider it to be a lifeline and the only thing that keeps you going.   Your health, finances, transportation, driver's license, and perhaps even your housing situation are affected if not entirely lost by now.

Love & Belonging

Your drug of choice or compulsive behavior has become your closest love relationship.   You can always depend on it to be there when you want it and it doesn't talk back.   More than likely you associate with others who have similar addictions as addicts don't usually like to use or be alone. At least those who behave similarly to you won't be nagging and complaining about your drinking/ using or other compulsive behavior.   Over time, isolating or even detaching from family, friends and associates may occur to avoid being seen using/ drinking/gambling, et cetera because others will start to complain and nag you.   If married, your spouse has either threatened to leave you or has already done so. Your children may have nothing to do with you and cut off all communication.

Power

One's need for Power in the form of appreciation from others and achievement is rarely met due to all of the crazy things that are said and done that push people away rather than provide the healthy needs of power. The addict's power will only come from his ability to score his or her drug in order to maintain his addiction. They feel unappreciated and disrespected because of all the things they say and do both when intoxicated and when sober. They rely on power to deal with others who are likewise using power by virtue of External Controlling behaviors of criticizing, blaming, complaining, nagging, threatening, punishing, and bribing or rewarding to get each other to behave the way they each want the other to behave. One who is addicted feels powerless to do anything to improve their unhappiness other than to get lost in their addiction.

Freedom

The only freedom drugs and alcohol, and other addictive behaviors create, is temporary freedom from their unwanted emotions and thoughts about their particular situation. There is little freedom when one is arrested for disorderly conduct, domestic violence, multiple DUI arrests, loss of employment, possessing or transporting drugs, stealing and robbing for money for drugs and alcohol.

Fun

The Addict/Alcoholic does not have fun in their life. They are spending most of their lives trying to override their unhappiness and physical discomfort with drugs or alcohol. Hangovers and medical conditions caused by drinking/using are not fun and often fatal. Living on the street is not fun. Having no income for food or shelter is not fun.

On the other hand, those addicted to non-substance addictive behaviors find fun in almost all that they do at the time of their addictive behavior. Their fun is acquired by the excitement of winning. At other times, they lack the experience of fun or pleasure and must then resort to the behavior that is missing when not doing the behavior. Their behavior often leads to the same losses of the addict/alcoholic: Loss of friends, family, finances, jobs, home, and lives.

What's Important To You Isn't Important To Everyone - Your Quality World

Another human trait we all have is a mental photo album of all of the things that are important to us that consists of our values, beliefs, places, things, expectations, friends, relatives, and the way we think everyone should behave, treat, and respect us. Dr. Glasser refers to this mental photo album as our **Quality World**. Our Quality World is at the core of our Internal Control system.

Happiness does not come from people, places, things, or situations that occur outside yourself in the external world. Your happiness is the result of your internal perception and thoughts regarding people, places, things, or situations. They either match the images and values you have in your Quality World or they don't. We humans are internally motivated rather than externally motivated.

Our perception of the Real World determines how we choose to react to it. We don't see the world as it really is. We see it as we are. Whatever makes up our attitudes, values, beliefs, wants, and personality will have an effect on how we see the world. No two people perceive the same things the same way. Reality is up for grabs. The substance dependent person sees the world through drug affected lenses. Nothing is really as it seems.

Whenever anything or anyone outside ourselves (the External World) sends us an image we perceive that doesn't match the image we possess in our Internal Quality World, we get a glitch and feel that something is out of balance. The natural tendency is to attempt to control the external image to make it match our internal image. This is where unhappiness begins. Trying to control others or things that cannot be controlled will only lead to disappointment, frustration, misery, and pain.

The only thing we can control is ourselves. Whenever we try to control others, we begin relying on External Control behaviors that harm our relationships . . . driving others away from us rather than bringing us closer together. External Control is an "I know what's better for you than you do" behavior.

Dr. Glasser states: *If everyone would realize that what is right for me does not make it right for everyone, the world would be a much happier place.*

There are also things in life besides people that we cannot control. They are what they are and nothing you can do or say will ever change them. No amount of worry, anxiety, stress, or tears will have any effect other than the effect it has over your emotional and physical wellbeing. Follow the words of Paul McCartney's mother Mary and "Let It Be." I recommend this approach several times throughout this book. Let it be.

Right now, the most important image in your Quality World is your drug or alcohol of choice, or your need for pleasure from gaming, sex, spending, et cetera. It must be noted that we are the only ones who can enter or remove any of the photo images we have in our Quality World. No one can do that for us. A counselor, doctor, friend, family member, or anyone else does not have the power to make that happen. Only you have the power to place the images of your happiness needs in your Quality World or remove them.

What this means is that your addictive behaviors that are affording you pleasure must be replaced with something of equal or greater value. This leads to the question of:

What's In It For Me?

A life of happiness, love, health, accomplishments, meaningful relationships, respect from others, financial freedom, and a world of exciting awareness are the things you can expect when you can rise above your addictions. More than likely, you have lost most, if not all, of these things that you once had. You would be only fooling yourself if you said you didn't want to have any of these things back in your life. You want to be happy again.

Go back and review the graph you did that indicates the things that are missing in your life and are keeping you from the happiness and life you want to have. Acquiring your Basic Needs and all the things you need for happiness is what's in it for you.

I'd Be Crazy To Choose To Be Addicted

Is there anyone who does not know that many drugs and alcohol are addictive? Unless you are extremely young or naive, everyone knows certain things to be addictive. At first, on the onset of drinking and using, a person believes that they will be able to notice whenever their use starts to become problematic, compulsive or addictive. As a result of this false belief, they choose to drink or use an addictive substance thinking they will stop at the first signs of addiction. Addictions are sneaky and insidious. Others will notice your addictive behaviors and problems long before you ever will. Meanwhile, the addictive behaviors are perceived as functioning normally to the addict. They have become spellbound by their drug/alcohol/medication.

While everyone knows drinking and drugs are addictive, no one purposely becomes addicted. Once they cross the line of bio-cellular addiction, it is no longer a choice. The use and abuse of alcohol and drugs are indeed a choice, but the addiction is something they didn't see coming and is not a choice.

Due to the reliance on the drug, or compulsive behavior, and the effects you experience by using, or doing them, you not only fail to recognize the symptoms of addiction but will also deny the symptoms exist or that you are addicted. You often become defensive whenever a family member or friend become concerned and mentions your drinking/using. If you don't think you have a problem, why do others think you do?

They aren't making things up. Why would they do so? They didn't say anything when it wasn't a problem. Here's another question for you. If *you* think you *might* have a problem, you most likely do. Otherwise, the thought would never cross your mind.

The same thing applies for non-substance addictive behaviors. If your compulsive uses of gambling, sexing, spending, eating disorders, et cetera are causing problems, then you are addicted. An anorexic individual continues to perceive themselves as overweight even when they have lost unhealthy amounts of weight. They feel powerless and begin to control their food intake giving them a sense of control. The most common symptom of substance and non-substance addiction is detaching from others and isolating. You didn't necessarily do this before you became engrossed in your compulsive behavior.

Admitting a problem exists is first and foremost a requirement in overcoming an addiction. Why make any effort to improve or make any changes in your life if you don't see your use as the cause of your unhappiness?

Am I Mentally Ill?

Not even close. People and professionals may consider you to have a mental disorder because of all the crazy things people say and do under the influence or dealing with intense frustration. There is no mental illness pathology for your addictive behaviors. Behavior is not a physical organ that can become ill or diseased. It is possible for the brain to be diseased but mental thoughts are not a brain or any other organ that can become physically affected with illness or disease.

Having been a counselor for over twenty-three years, I can tell you that not one of my clients ever came to see me because they couldn't deal with all the happiness in their life. Their commonality is: They are unhappy and their unhappiness is the result of unsatisfying relationships. They have unsatisfying relationships with those important to them or they have no relationships at all. Their addictions and/or other *crazy-like* behaviors are the result of their creativity and the choices they make to deal with their unhappiness. They are attempting to get the image they have of their unhappy relationship to match the wanted image they have in their Quality World. . . and nothing they have tried is working.

The behaviors of those who have been labeled schizophrenic, Bi-polar, Obsessive Compulsive, Dissociative Personality Disorder; suffer from Anxiety, Depression, et al have no pathology as the cause of their behavior. Every client I have had the fortune to see had the same underlying problem regardless of the mental illness label they had been given. They all had unsatisfying relationships. Mental illness diagnoses are made based only on subjective observations. There are no objective tests or confirmable abnormalities of the brain for most of those so-called mental illnesses listed in the Diagnostic and Statistical Manual of Mental Disorders. (DSM).

These diagnoses are made based upon opinions made by a group of collective "experts" who agreed on the behaviors to identify them. It is diagnoses by decree.iii

When you see your doctor for a physical illness, several tests are made such as EKGs for heart conditions, blood tests for several possible conditions, X-rays, CT scans, MRIs and many other tests that indicate pathology to the cause and source of one's illness. Whenever a psychiatrist and/or medical doctor make a mental illness diagnosis, there are no objective tests. They come to a conclusion of a mental disorder based upon subjective information given by the client or others, and/or by observed behaviors.

How many people would start a chemotherapy program or insulin treatment for cancer or diabetes because a doctor told them that they look and behave like someone who has cancer or diabetes? Yet doctors and psychiatrists are prescribing drugs that have no curative abilities, for conditions that have no pathology. These drugs not only fail to cure a non-existent medical condition, they also cause the brain to function differently than it is naturally supposed to function. They often cause permanent damage to the brain and even lead to crimes against others and suicide.

The real danger of these psychoactive medications is their addiction. Once these drugs are started , it will require medical supervision to gradually stop their use. I have interviewed several clients on this medication who praise it to no end. I have been told that they would rather suffer the bad effects of the drug than deal with their anxiety. They have

iii O'Meara, Kelly Patricia, "Psyched Out," Author House, Bloomington, IN, 2006 become spellbound by the drug's effects and acquired a vicious addiction to just one of many addictive prescription medications that are being prescribed by doctors and psychiatrists.

Dr. Peter Breggin states:

Spellbinding often occurs rapidly in an overwhelming fashion, often within the first few doses of a psychoactive drug. However, especially in regard to tranquilizers and sleeping pills, spellbinding can occur gradually, creeping up on the individual over time. Eventually the individual becomes completely disabled without having any idea what happened. The victim of medication spellbinding can become desperately drug dependent, easily manipulated, emotionally unstable, depressed, and suicidal.[iv]

In all the cases of mass shootings, the perpetrators were, or had been, taking psychiatric medications.[v] Hardly anyone is associating the behavior to be a result of the medications they were taking or had been taking. Instead, society wants to blame the behavior on some brain abnormality that has never been discovered in the autopsies of these shooters. They are also generally young men (not women) between the ages of 15 and 25.

No drug has the ability to focus on any one unwanted or problematic emotion without it affecting *all* emotions. Both prescription and

---

[iv] Breggin, Peter, MD, 'Medication Madness," p. 167, St. Martin's Press, NY, 2008

[v] Mike Adams, https://www.naturalnews.com/039752_mass_shootings_psychiatric_drugs_antidepressants.html

illegal drugs harm the brain's normal creative ability to effectively find better solutions for one's unhappiness. By numbing the brain and interfering with its normal functioning, a client may feel better because their brain is drugged. They become addicted to these medications in the very same way as alcohol and other drugs. They like how they make them feel.

Anyone who has been relying on drugs and/or alcohol for several months or years has been taking substances that alter the mind's creative and normal functioning abilities. In order to make an accurate diagnosis, it should be conducted when there are no longer any traces of alcohol or drugs in the body and brain. Otherwise, they would be evaluating drug-affected behavior. It may take as much as 30 days or more before such a mental diagnosis can be made. Once a person is totally free of chemical elements, it has been found that alcoholics and addicts have no more psychological issues than that of the non-addicted populations.

If you are currently taking any psychiatric medication for depression, anxiety, schizophrenia, or any other behavior medication, do not cease using them without medical supervision. The two most dangerous times to take these drugs are when you first start taking them and when you stop taking them. The effects can be quite serious.

Drugs don't have side effects. They have effects.

Mental Illness labels are given to those who are only doing the best they can with what they know to do to satisfy their Basic Needs. Why do some people choose depressing, anxieting, obsessing, Bipolarizing, and most all other behaviors being called mental illness? Why do some people choose one type of unnatural behavior over another? When feeling powerless and frustrated, and after everything they tried to feel better has failed, they use their creativity to invent any number of several ways in which to feel better and gain control. Whatever they discovered first that gave them some sense of control and easement of frustration is why they don't invent or choose other behaviors to get the desired effect. If they didn't choose these behaviors, they would feel more powerless, frustrated, and out of control of their lives.

A client once told me, "I would have to be out of my right mind to choose mental illness behaviors." As a certified mental health counselor, I would have to agree. No one ever made an appointment with me because they were in their right mind.

Why Would I Choose To Depress?

This is an excellent question and my response will also apply to many other so-called mental illness behaviors. Depression, like all other behaviors, is purposeful. All our behaviors serve a purpose in our attempts to get our Basic Needs met and acquire happiness or pleasure. The purpose to choose to depress is one's best attempt at the time to deal with an unhappy relationship or not having any relationships at all.

1. Choosing to depress can be a way to get help from others without having to outright ask for it.

While you may not personally know me, if I were depressing, you would notice it by my facial expression, downcast look, tone of voice, and body language. You might easily come up to me and ask, "Mike, are you okay?" I just got concern and help without asking for it.

2.   Choosing to depress will keep you from choosing to feel angry. You cannot be angry and depressed at the same time. Anger is expressing your unhappiness outwardly.   Depression is expressing your unhappiness inwardly. Those who don't wish to feel anger, or who may be fearful of what they might do in their state of anger, choose to depress to avoid their anger.

3. Choosing to depress, as well as many other so-called mental illness behaviors, is a means of controlling other people.   Parents, spouses, siblings, students, and employers can be very artful in the act of depressing to get others to do what they want them to do.

4. The next reason people choose to depress (and other behaviors) is their refusal to accept the reality of a given situation and/or they know they have to do something about a problem and:

> a. They don't want to do it.
>
> b. They don't know how to do it.

These are the reasons why anyone would choose to depress or behave in other abnormal ways. Addicted individuals may employ all four reasons; however, the one that gets the most use is reason number four.   You deny you have a problem yet subconsciously, you know that you do.   You just don't want to accept it. And if you ever do accept the reality of your addiction, you know you have to stop and you don't want to and only know one way to stop (cold turkey) and you don't want to go through the pain of withdrawal symptoms.

What this all boils down to is fear. You know what to expect if you continue with your behavior even though it causes you problems. What frightens you is not knowing what to expect or what will happen if you give it up. If nothing changes, nothing will change.

The guidelines I offer you in this book and the concept of Choice Theory are sure to give you your life back and on the road to the happiness you wish you had. What I can't guarantee is that you will utilize this information. This book is only information and information will only be as effective is if you use it in a way that is more effective than what you have been doing. The guarantee is only granted to the person who follows the concepts . . . you. If you don't trust my words and the concepts of Dr. Glasser's Choice Theory, you will not get your needs met. Trust us. Like many addicts, you have lost important relationships, finances, jobs, and more. Your losses will eventually result in the loss of your life. You have everything to gain and not much more to lose.

3. Choice Theory in Action

What is keeping you from being happy?

Whatever it is, your unhappiness is something that is happening right now . . . in the present. It may have begun several years ago but the problem is happening right now. Whatever happened years ago may very well be why you chose to start drinking or using drugs but it has nothing to do with your ability to do something about it now, today. Whatever happened in the past is done. It's over. You can't change whatever it is that happened no matter how hard you try. All you can control is to take measures to find the happiness you want right now and from now on.

Staying in the past keeps you in the role of a victim. It freezes you in time and keeps you from growth. It causes you to feel sorry for yourself as well as remorseful for any of the things you have said and done while under the influence that harmed your relationships with the important people in your life. You also resent and feel wounded by the things said and done to you by others either real or imagined. As a victim you feel sorry for yourself and think, "Poor me. Poor me. Pour me another drink." If we focus on the behavior and symptoms, we avoid focusing on the cause.

I'm often asked by my clients why I don't inquire about their past and what happened to them long ago. They feel somewhat short-changed if I don't have them discuss their unhappy past. They appear to want to know "why" certain things happened to them. You may know why your tooth aches but it will still ache until you see a dentist and do something about it. Knowledge of causes doesn't dissipate a problem. Effective treatment does. Another reason why I don't deal with the past is because when clients leave my office, I want them to feel better than they did when they came in. Talking about an unhappy past can only reinforce one's unhappiness.

The effectiveness of Reality Therapy is that we listen to, but don't focus on the pain or the symptom. Instead, the goal is to remedy unsatisfying relationships, or find better relationships, as well as developing better coping skills to deal with unsatisfying relationships.

If you want to reflect on the past, recall the time in your life before you began drinking or drugging or other addictive behavior. You had more friends, were happier, and enjoyed life far more than you have been lately. You weren't having any major relationship issues.

You found out a long time ago that drinking, drugging, or other compulsive behaviors gave you better control over your unhappiness than anything else you could think of at the time. Relying on these behaviors progressed while easing the frustration of your unsatisfying relationship(s). All the alcohol and drugs in the world will not be effective in helping someone improve their relationships. Choice Theory is a method to regain control of your life as well as discover more healthy and effective ways to get your basic happiness needs met.

What Do You Want? How Do You Want Your Life To Be Different Than It Is Right Now?

If your life were ideally the way you would like it to be in your Quality World, how would it be different than it is right now?

Who would be in your Quality World? What are their names? What is their relationship to you? What emotions would you be feeling if your relationship with them is where you would like it to be?

If you were no longer addicted, who would be the first person you would want to know about your sobriety?

Don't just read and answer these questions silently. Write them down and answer them one by one. Then visualize them in your mind as if you were currently in possession of these wants. Doing so will give you a fairly good picture of the way you want your life to be. How would you look? How would you feel if everything was in place for your desired life?

Do the people in your Quality World have you in their Quality World or have they removed you from it because of things you have said and done while drinking/using?

Who are the people that you would like to put you back in their Quality World? You can't control them to get them to put you back in their Quality

World, but you can control yourself by making changes that could cause them to want you back in their life. Since the only person you can control is yourself, there are no guarantees that others may have a change of heart. It's easy to find someone to love. Findings someone to love you back is the hard part . . . especially if you have created a lot of wreckage in both of your lives from your addictions.

Take the time to write down the answer to all of the above questions and pore over them. Don't be in a hurry to follow these exercises for a quick fix. There is no such thing as fast recovery. Your addiction and behaviors were developed over a long period of time and there is no overnight cure. It's a process that requires you to do some serious soul searching and experience possible sad emotions. But remember . . . you have a choice to feel sad or some other emotion when doing this exercise.

If you choose to feel emotional about these, choose anger rather than sadness or depressing. Your anger can be a motivator to take action and get your life back to where you want it to be and beyond. But don't linger on it. Make sure your anger is self-directed so as not to take it out on others. As a caveat: Too much self-directed anger can lead to adding lower self-worth and relying on your drug of choice to feel better. Don't kick your ass when so many others have already done it for you.

Focus and concentrate on these questions daily, several times a day, for at least two or three days. If you have a sponsor in any 12 step groups you may be attending (I highly recommend doing so) ask them to listen to your wants and how you want things to be with the important people in your life. If you don't attend support groups or have a sponsor, then find a person you trust who is willing to listen to you and validate your wants and the way you would like things to be without judging or criticizing you.

What Have You Been Doing To Acquire Those Things You Want In Your Quality World?

Several years ago, Dr. Phil (McGraw) asked Dr. Glasser to be on his board of directors for his TV show. It was through this connection that Dr. Phil took a line from Choice Theory and adopted the phrase, "How's that workin' for ya?" said in his Oklahoma drawl. Self evaluation is part of the Reality Therapy and Choice Theory concepts that takes a look at a person's choices to find happiness. Only we use the phrase, "How effective have your methods been in getting you what you want?"

Whatever you have been doing hasn't been working. So why keep on doing what doesn't work? What are some things you haven't done to overcome your addictions? Most likely, you have tried a few times on your own to stop. You have been your own treatment agency telling everyone that you can deal with your own issues and don't need anybody's help, and you can do it on your own. If your methods to stop on your own and find happiness were effective, you would have stopped a long time ago.

If you're like most people who suffer from compulsive behaviors, you haven't been doing much of anything to get what you want other than your choices that have been keeping you from getting what you want. I would, however, dare say that you have made a few attempts to quit on your own. What happened each time you tried to quit and failed? What was going on in your life that stressed you to the point of relapsing? Was it because you were feeling sick and irritable from withdrawal symptoms? Perhaps someone said or did something that set you back when you chose to react to it the way you did. It could also be your own self talk and perception of your own low self-worth and you relapsed just to escape your unwanted and unhappy emotions. Whatever it was, it was situational, emotional, and/or physical.

Victor Frankl reminds us, "*Between stimulus and response, there is a space. In that space is our power to choose how we react to it.*"

The Shame and Guilt Spiral

All individuals addicted to drugs or alcohol have two things in common: Shame and Guilt. This is because of all the things they have said and done in their addicted lives. The concept of Guilt is: "I *did* something wrong." The concept of Shame is: "I *am* something wrong." These two perceptions are enough to drive anyone to compulsive behaviors. Once locked into the shame and guilt spiral, addicts resort to continued or even heavier drinking/using/ or other compulsive behaviors to escape these unwanted perceptions of self. When they sober up, they criticize themselves even more for having used and that only adds more shame and guilt. They lead a life in a shame and guilt spiral that often leads to total despair and even suicide.

The more you rely on compulsive addictive behaviors to overcome your unhappiness, the more you will become unhappy. The more unhappy you become, the more you rely on compulsive addictive behaviors.   The more you rely on compulsive addictive behaviors, the more you will detach from others.   Ironically, your addictive behaviors to find happiness are destroying the very things you want and need to be happy . . . meaningful relationships with the important people in your life.

Your Creative Mind

When faced with adversity and unsatisfying situations, we rely on our creativity to "fix it" and make it better.   Over the years, we have learned and created many different ways we solved our unhappiness.   Some tools worked and many of them failed and made things worse.   It all goes back to the previous concept I wrote earlier about making unpleasant situations more acceptable and trying to make the external image match the internal image we have in our Quality World.   Your creativity is your way of attempting to make the outside perception match your internal image of what and how you want things to be.

If none of the tools we have to find happiness are successful, we become inventors . . . creating new tools (behaviors) to fix a problem when all else has failed.   Some of these creative behaviors people create can be pretty far out or unusual to the point that others may observe the behavior and think they are mentally ill.   While many creative behaviors may seem strange to others, the inventor sees them as making complete and total sense at the time.   It's one's best choice at the time to make an unhappy situation better.

There are all sorts of creative behaviors such as depressing, anxieting, schizophrenicing, obsessing, aching, gambling, sexing, excessive spending just to name a few. If you wonder why I ended many of these behaviors with "ing," it's because they are behaviors. Behaviors are actions and actions are verbs or gerunds.   These are behaviors one chooses when everything else they have tried to find happiness and to satisfy their basic needs have failed.   The behaviors may not fully be totally successful at resolving their unhappiness but they do, to some degree, lessen their frustration and unhappiness at the time they do them.   People do whatever works for them or they wouldn't do it.   Other people often can't and don't see how it is working for them.   The inability of others to see a person's unusual behavior as having a benefit to the person doing them often leads to concluding that the person is mentally ill.

The oldest tried, tested, and relied upon creative behavior that many choose to deal with their unhappiness is drugs and alcohol or other compulsive behaviors.   While creating a sense of euphoria and numbing the brain, you feel less unhappy and feel some bit of pleasure. The reason why this choice is so common is because it works and works fast to temporarily mask the unhappiness.   The problem, however, is that after sobering up or stopping the addictive behavior, the problem still exists so the need to drink/use/

behave must be repeated to experience the wanted effect.

Use your creativity to think of ways that might work better and cause fewer problems. Try them out. If something doesn't work, create another possible behavior that might help you meet your happiness needs in healthier and more productive ways.

Need Some Help or Ideas?

Go to Alcoholics Anonymous, Cocaine Anonymous, Narcotics Anonymous, Gamblers Anonymous, Sexaholics Anonymous, or other support groups such as Rational Recovery, Smart Recovery, Lifering, Women For Sobriety, et al. There are support groups for every imaginable situation that affects one's ability to find happiness. They are also free and cost nothing but your time and attendance. Use Internet resources to locate them in your area. Get a sponsor.

Go to church. Renew your connection with your faith that you may have given up.

Locate and meet with a counselor, preferably one who is certified in Choice Theory. But at this stage of your life, any counselor is better than no counselor. There are other Cognitive Behavioral Therapists available. Ask them if they utilize Cognitive Behavioral Therapy (CBT) methods in their practice.

Avoid associating with any and all of your drinking friends. You might respond, "Then I wouldn't have any friends at all." Not surprising. You can find new friends in support groups. These groups are called "fellowships" for a reason.

Avoid any people in your life that are toxic or create anxiety, anger, arguments, et cetera. Sometimes, the people who are closest to us are the most toxic to us. Turn your back on them and walk away and learn something about yourself and after a period of comfortable sobriety, return to them and see if you both have learned anything. Don't be surprised to discover that you are the only one who may have learned anything while apart. Just don't fall in the trap of their external controlling methods and resentment of your past behavior. If not, you may have to divorce yourself from them on a somewhat permanent basis. Sometimes this involves your family. Your happiness and sobriety depends on it.

Get with your sponsor or counselor and discuss other possible creative ways to take back control of your life without addictions.

Read Dr. Glasser's book, "Take Charge Of Your Life"

Replace your addictive substance with another non-toxic substance or behavior, i.e. a non-alcoholic beverage, gum, exercise, sports, school, hobbies, enjoyable recreations, music, writing, art.

Create anything that works to overcome your addictive urges and behavior that does not cause any further problems. I have always said, "If someone were to tell me that they were able to overcome their addiction by standing on their head every time they felt the urge to drink/use, I would say, go for it."

4. What If I Don't Like AA or Any of Those Twelve Step Groups?

I will be the first to tell you that AA is not for everyone. It is, however, what works best for most. Those who have trouble with AA are those who really don't want to overcome their addictions and give up their use. Others have difficulty dealing with "the God thing." Those who do not have much of a religious background find it difficult to relate. AA is not a religion but it does involve a Higher Power. The advantage to those who do have a belief is that they use God as someone to give them strength and courage to struggle through their road to sobriety and a better life. They rely on their faith that a higher power can get them through the long process of recovery by way of the unconditional love, and acceptance of a higher power who gives them strength to face their problems today and have hope for tomorrow.

Others see AA as only a group of people who sit around and do nothing but talk about the past and what they experienced. Their drug affected thinking fails their ability to actually see what purpose these stories have. They are meant to describe and share all of the things they did and said in their drunken or drug affected lives. They are admitting the "sins of their ways." Sooner or later, someone's story will hit home to someone in the group and cause an "ah ha" moment of understanding.

Choice Theory is very AA compatible but there is no reference to religion. Choice Theory leads clients to find their inner strengths and develop their own healthy coping skills to overpower the urge to drink/use or other compulsive behaviors. By learning Internal Control psychology, the events of External Control situations are dealt with in peaceful and calm ways.

There are other support groups besides AA that are non-secular. I highly recommend support groups for the following reason: You will be with others who know full-well what you are going through. They've been there. They can help you out of the hole you are in. They offer support when it may seem that no one cares. They address your issues without criticizing, blaming, and judging you like others have. They don't cost anything.

Having a sponsor is advantageous as it gives you someone with whom you trust and can bare your soul to. Your sponsor may be the only person who truly understands you. Right now, you may need all the friends you can get because many of those in the past have walked away from you for all the things you have said and done. Non-using/drinking/compulsive support group members make the best friends you could possibly have right now. They, too, are not judgmental and for the most part they don't rely on external controlling behaviors.

There's More To Your Behavior Than You Realize

Total Behavior, another element of Choice Theory, is made up of four separate components. Two of these components are things that you have the direct capability to control. The other two you have indirect control. Those that you can directly control are your Thinking and your Behavior. You can totally control your thoughts and your behavior. To do so is a choice. You choose everything that you do. All you do from birth until death is behave and all your behavior is purposeful to satisfy happiness or pleasure. The behaviors you choose to satisfy your basic needs are a conscious choice based upon past successful applications, learned/observed from others, or newly invented behaviors when all else has failed.

By controlling your thinking and/or behavior, you indirectly control the other two components of Total Behavior . . . your Emotions and Physiology. Whatever you choose to think or do will have subsequent effects on your emotions and your physiology.

Even the misery and unhappiness that you choose to experience is difficult to maintain when you realize that you have a choice on how you want to feel and behave. Whatever you may be feeling is the direct result of what you perceive and think about the situation and how you choose to behave to deal with it. You cannot have an emotion, happy or unhappy, without a thought preceding the emotion. It's impossible. Whatever you are thinking will result in an emotion based upon what you perceive is going on outside yourself. People, places, things, and situations don't "make" you have negative or positive emotions. You choose them. Your emotions are solely the result of your thoughts about what you perceive in the outside world that doesn't match the images in your Quality World. You *always* have a choice on how to respond to them.

If the front wheels of your car represent your thoughts and behavior, then imagine that your back wheels represent your feelings and physiology. If you turn your front wheels to the left, your back wheels have to follow. Likewise, if you turn your front wheels to the right, your back wheels must follow. Therefore, however you control your front wheels, determines how your rear wheels will respond.

Once you fully understand this component of Total Behavior, and all the components of Choice Theory, you will find just how simple it is to take control of any given unwanted situation and find the happiness and serenity you so dearly want to have. You will have complete control of your life when you utilize one or more of only three simple and easy choices when faced with adversity and unhappiness.

Here are your 3 choices:

1. Change what you want (your thinking).

2. Change how you behave when you don't get what you want (acting/behavior).

3. Change both your wants and behavior.

Want to avoid unwanted emotions and situations? Change what you are thinking or what you are doing. Want others to behave the way you want them to behave? Change what you want and stop expecting others to behave the way you want them to behave. Want to improve your relationships? Stop using the external controlling behaviors of criticizing, blaming, complaining, nagging, threatening, punishing, and bribing or rewarding to get them to do what you want them to do. When others apply these controlling behaviors on you, you always have a choice on how to react to them. Want to break away from your so-called mental illness labels and behaviors including addictions? Do all of the above. Read Dr. William Glasser's book, "Choice Theory" and other books listed in the bibliography of this book.

5. Overcoming Your Addiction

Before You Begin

You already expect me to say "Stop Drinking/Using" or any other compulsive behavior. No, I'm not going to tell you to do that yet for two reasons:

1. Assess the severity of your substance abuse or compulsive behavior first.

2. You will have a better chance of success toward recovery if you know what to expect before you start.

What Are Your Withdrawal Symptoms?

If you've tried to quit before, you can recognize some of the following withdrawal symptoms. The most common withdrawal effects after stopping the use of drugs or alcohol is a sense of anxiety, nervousness, depression, difficulty getting to sleep, poor concentration, and edginess. With that may come irritability with people and unexpected situations. These can almost be guaranteed experiences. Your first thoughts may be to have a drink or use just to alleviate those symptoms. That's how you've always done it for perhaps years. But don't. Ride it out instead. These symptoms will last only a few minutes at a time for a few days and in some cases, a couple of weeks and occasional reemergence for several months but less often.

Next, dependent on the substance you have been taking, you may have sleep problems. While drinking, your intake has interfered with the oxygen supply that goes to your brain resulting in passing out, and affecting your respiration. Now your brain is trying to adjust to the change of not being drug affected. This, too, is dependent upon the seriousness of your use and how long you have been relying on your drug and alcohol of choice.

Once your brain and body adjust to the absence of alcohol or drug, you will begin to get more restful sleep. You may also begin to have very lucid dreams and many of them may be of you drinking or using. Some of your dreams can seem so real that you wake up believing the scenario actually existed. Getting deeper sleep, or REM sleep, is when dreams occur. Incidentally, some of your dreams can be pretty far out and "crazy." This is merely your brain being creative while you sleep. If it can be creative while you sleep, it is also capable of being creative in like manner when you are awake.

More serious withdrawal symptoms may involve diarrhea, headaches, sweating, and nausea. With opiate withdrawal, you will experience severe aches and pains especially in your back and generally all over. Again, these are things that commonly lead to relapse because returning to the drug/alcohol will make these symptoms dissipate. Depending on the severity of these symptoms, you may opt to get a medically supervised detoxification program in an inpatient client or in a hospital for three to ten days before proceeding with recovery.

The most serious withdrawal symptoms include severe shakes, hallucinations, becoming delirious, vomiting, striking out at others, seizures, diarrhea, and/or chest pains. Symptoms of this nature require definite medical supervision in an inpatient setting.

These are just a few of the withdrawal symptoms you may expect to experience. You don't have to experience all of them for your addiction to be considered serious. Any one or more symptoms are to be considered serious. I don't advise outpatient treatment for the more serious withdrawal symptoms by any means. It could be the difference between life and death.

Read This Book More Than Once Before Starting Recovery

You have been drugging your body and brain for some period of time now and you may be experiencing some degree of cognitive dissonance. In other words, you may not be focusing and processing too well on the information contained in this book. The more you read it, the more you will pick up on things that were easily overlooked in previous readings.

I once thought I knew all there was to know about Choice Theory because I read Dr. Glasser's book and I was completely sober when I did so. I didn't realize how uneducated I was about it, even after having read the book, until I attended several training sessions and lectures conducted by Dr. Glasser and re-read his book a few more times.

I also recommend you read this book several times during your recovery process. There is a bibliography at the end of this book for more suggested reading. There are also many other sources of reading material to help you along the way. You can research them via Google, Amazon, or your library. The more you contribute and take action, the more you increase your ability to attain complete recovery.

Of all the components of Choice Theory, I primarily center on your Quality World in dealing with addictions; satisfying your Basic Needs for happiness; and your Total Behavior. The other components will also be involved by adding and augmenting these primary components.

Accept The Reality of Your Addiction

Now I'll say it: "Stop drinking, using, or whatever other compulsive behavior you have been doing."

Thinking and Behaving are things you can control that will indirectly affect your unwanted emotions and physical well-being. Empty and throw out anything in your home that contains alcohol or drugs . . . including prescription meds, unless you have been prescribed them for a current and specific medical condition. Toss out anything and everything you may have stashed away or hidden "just in case" or for an "emergency." If you are on antidepressant and ant- anxiety meds, or other psych meds, don't stop taking them without medical supervision and gradually reducing your dosage. Peter Breggin describes the spellbinding aspects of addiction to psych meds mirroring those of other substance abuse addictions.

Be ready for the emotional and physical withdrawal symptoms mentioned earlier. Overcoming your urges to drink or use can be overridden by *changing your thinking and current behavior* when experiencing these urges. Stop thinking about wanting to drink or use a drug (or other compulsive behavior). Choose not to take action and opt instead to experience and endure a short-lasting urge to drink or use or other compulsive behavior. Changing your thoughts and behavior will cause your urges to pass in a relatively short period of time. Rely on this method as often as you experience the urges to use or behave.

Do something different than you are doing at the moment. Take a walk, go to the gym, jog, drink your favorite soft drink, go to a 12-step meeting, and if you have a sponsor . . . call them and tell them what you are feeling and thinking. They will understand and help you through the urge to drink/ use. If you don't have a sponsor, call someone and tell them that you need to talk to them to fight off your urges to drink/use. Refer back to the chapter on Creativity.

Few people have only one addiction. The most common additional addiction that goes along with alcohol or drugs is nicotine. If you are a smoker, I would advise against any attempt to stop this addiction at the same time as your primary addiction. Doubling up on withdrawal symptoms lessens your ability to successfully overcome your primary addiction. However, I have seen it successfully done by highly self-controlling individuals. I'm only suggesting you deal with one addiction at a time so as not to add more stress than you may already have while ceasing your primary addiction.

Alcohol, drugs, or any of the other non-substance addictive behaviors are in your Quality World. You are the only person who can take them out but you will need to replace them with something similar or more pleasant and less harmful and life-controlling. I replaced my drinking with Iced Tea. I drank copious amounts after my initial abstinence from alcohol. A few years later, I replaced my cigarette habit with pure air, better health, and more money in my pocket. Of the two addictions, stopping the cigarette habit was far more difficult for me than stopping my alcohol abuse . . . and alcohol abstinence was not easy. I had a forty-three-year history of smoking. In both cases, I had to change my thinking about drinking and smoking in order to help control my behavior of practicing my habit. Incidentally, I failed to stop smoking several times before I actually succeeded.

Mark Twain remarked, "Giving up smoking is the easiest thing in the world. I know because I've done it thousands of times."

By focusing on the benefits of not drinking or smoking more so than how much I wanted them was helpful in fighting the urges to drink or smoke. Remind yourself often of what you have to gain by giving up your addiction.

Here are some benefits to get you started:

Better relationships with family, friends, and yourself

Happiness

Gainful employment

Financial income

Acquiring your Basic Genetic Needs of:

    Survival

    Love and Belonging

    Power

    Freedom

    Fun

Improved health and less illness

More recognized opportunities to improve your life.

Restful sleep

Who and What Is In Your Quality World?

Who are the most important people in your life? Write their names down on a piece of paper. Then place a number from 1 to 5 based upon how important you value them.   Then write after each number of importance, write down a number from 0 to 5 how happy you are with your relationship with them and/or they with you.

Incidentally, you don't have to use the numbers 1 to 5 in numerical order.   You can use the same number several times.   The same applies when completing the ratings of importance in your Basic Need graph in the earlier chapter.

What can you do for the sake of your relationship to improve your situation with those who have a low satisfactory number rating? Use your Creativity to try to improve your relationship with them that you have not tried before. If something doesn't work, invent more options to improve your relationship. There may be times when you know what to do to improve the relationship but you don't want to do it. Do it anyway.

What are your values about those things that you consider to be right for you? How do you want things to be? How do you want others to treat you? How do you want to treat others? How much do you live up to your own values? Do you walk your talk? Do you expect others to live by the same values you think is right for you? If so, who gave you that authority? If so, what problems has this concept caused you in your relationships with others? Just because it may be right for you does not mean it is right for anyone else.

How successful have you been in convincing others to remove their values and beliefs from their Quality World? Better yet, how successful have others been to get you to remove your values and beliefs from your own Quality World? The answer will be a resounding "None." However, I'm sure you have taken other people out of your Quality World and others have taken you out of theirs.

Why try to control others to get them to do what you want them to do that will cause either of you to take each other out of your Quality Worlds? Has controlling others brought you closer together or distanced your relationship with them?

What else in your Quality World have you possibly lost? Have you lost your employment, family, home, transportation, health, material possessions? What caused the loss of any one or more of them? What can you do to get them back? Does drinking, using, or hours of gaming or other compulsive behaviors bring you closer to what you want in life or do they make it more difficult to attain, if at all? Make a plan and follow up with it. If one plan doesn't work, make another plan. How effective do you think that overcoming your addiction would be if you acquired whatever you may have lost?

I am not asking rhetorical questions. Take several days to ponder and answer all the above questions. Begin writing and putting your thoughts into words one question at a time in order to bring them into more conscious awareness. Keep a journal or start your own self-help awareness book. Don't hurry this process. It has taken years for you to develop these addictive habits and past choices. They won't get better overnight.

Acquiring Meaningful Relationships

As simplistic as that may sound, meaningful relationships are the core of finding happiness and getting your basic needs met so that you can maintain sobriety. The process requires recognizing what's in your Quality World and the things that are important to you; your perception of things outside yourself, and ways of dealing with things in the Real World; eliminating External Controlling behaviors that you and everyone else in your life have been relying on to deal with other people; understanding your Basic Needs that are behind all the things you do and need to have in order to   acquire happiness;   understanding that you choose all of your emotions, behaviors and misery; how you use your creativity and invent behaviors when all else fails; and finally: Utilizing Total Behavior to find happiness, peace of mind, and reclaim your life.

Dr. Glasser tells us that all long-term emotional problems are relationship problems. Someone important to you is not behaving the way you would like them to behave. You are not having the relationship that you would like to have with someone important to you or you may not have any relationships at all. In fact, you, yourself, may be the person who is behaving in ways in which you disapprove. Since you have no control over others, you definitely have the ability to control yourself.

If someone were to ask why all of your friends are gone, what would you say?   What is it that you have been doing of which they disapproved? People don't leave other people because they like them. What is it that causes others to stop liking you?   Why did you stop liking them?   Did they threaten your way of surviving by your use of drugs, alcohol, or other compulsive behavior?   An addict's attitude, behavior, and things said to the important people in their life tend to push others away. The external control of others to get you to change or stop your behavior has pushed you away from them.

Stop Using External Control

You   started   drinking/using   or   other   behaviors because you were unhappy. Doing so eased your frustration and unhappiness at the time you indulged. As strange as it may seem, it also gave you a sense of control when you felt you had no control in your life. The behavior you chose was only effective as long as you did them so you did it often. This led to compulsive behavior and/or bio-cellular addiction. And while you were busy drinking/using or other addictive behavior, the skills and life's lessons you were supposed to learn in life passed you by. You failed to acquire good relationships skills and how to effectively deal with stress and anger, and ways to resolve conflict with others without anger and resentment.

What led to your unhappiness is/was the loss or lack of any meaningful relationships and what you were thinking about them at the time. Outside of losing your home or loved ones to fire, flood, tornados or hurricanes, or living in poverty or in a war-torn area, the most common cause of any of your past unhappiness was a problem you were having with someone important to you. Reflect back on all of the times you were depressed. Each instance involved a problem with someone else.

Unsatisfying relationships cause unhappiness. Unhappiness leads to choosing behaviors to control the situation to provide happiness or to distract from your sorrow. Since you can only control yourself, trying to control a situation involving another person almost always fails. Even if a controlling method did result in getting what you wanted, it severely harmed your relationship with that person. You made several creative attempts to try to match the image in the External World to those in your Quality Internal World and still nothing worked. What did work to some extent was relying on drugs/alcohol or other compulsive behavior to ease the frustration and unhappiness of failed attempts for a meaningful relationship. Addiction is a false panacea for unhappiness that only leads to more unhappiness.

Since the lack of meaningful relationships are at the core of addiction, compulsive use, and other behaviors, then acquiring meaningful relationships is what can overcome these behaviors. It's not as easy as it sounds because now, we have the physical bio-cellular aspect to deal with as well. As difficult as it may be, those with non-substance addictions may find it easier than the drug and alcohol addicted person for changing behavior.

I highly recommend you acquire a friendship with someone of the same gender who has several years of being clean and sober and also with another person who has never had a drug, alcohol, or other addiction. You will benefit from both of these two people who will have lots of help in guiding you on your road to recovery. You have much to learn from hanging with recovering people and those who have never had an addiction problem . . . "normies." Normies know how to live without drugs, alcohol, or other compulsive behaviors.

Romantic Relationships

If you are in a current romantic relationship, continue to the next topic of Slippery Slope. If not in a current romantic relationship, don't begin seeking one, at least for now. Your relationships will only be as healthy as you are now. It will take years to begin to recognize all of the things about you and your interaction with others because you will not be able to see them all at one time. The more you learn and grow, the more you will be able to recognize the things that often get in the way of maintaining a healthy relationship. Start visualizing yourself from the point of view of others instead of your own internal self-visualization. Listen to the things you say. If you had met someone just like you, how well would you like that person? The more you see the need to make personal changes in your life, the better you will be able to find healthier relationships.

If someone calls you a horse's ass, that's merely their opinion. But if two or more people call you a horse's ass, perhaps it's time to shop for a saddle.

While there is no specific time period to establish before cultivating a romantic relationship, I recommend at least two years getting to know you better before becoming romantically involved. Again, that's a choice you will have to make when you feel ready more than you may feel needy. After several years, I am still questioning some of my behaviors and interactions with others. Self-evaluation is an important and on-going part of recovery.

A Slippery Slope

You aren't going to like what I am about to tell you. Some of the current friends in your life are those who bonded with you and kept you from feeling alone when everyone else in your life left you, or you left them. Others tried to control you and your addiction so you took them out of your Quality World and replaced them with those who behaved similarly to you. No one with an addiction likes to use or drink alone. They associate with others with similar addictions that don't judge them or criticize them.

It's time to let them go. You may feel they are all you have but trust me . . . they are not good for you or your recovery. Here is where it becomes important for you to make new friends who have been where you are but currently in recovery. You will be able to relate to them and they will be healthy support and strength for your own sobriety. Yes, I'm once again referencing A.A. or other support groups. Again, I want to remind you . . . you can't do this alone.

Similarly, don't return to your regular locations where you gathered to drink or use even though you tell yourself that you won't be using or drinking when you go there. Familiar people and surroundings only offer triggers that lead to relapsing.

After a year of abstinence, and avoiding my old drinking hangouts and friends, I made the choice to "go see the old gang." I walked into the bar where we all used to meet and there, at the same corner of the bar, were all those same faces and people with whom I used to drink and associate.

A year had passed and they were still situated at the same location like Norm on the TV show Cheers. They all reveled as they recognized me and asked where I had been keeping myself. Several asked, "Buy you a drink?" I said, "Sure. I'll have an iced tea." They immediately recoiled and one of them told me to do something that was physically impossible to do of a sexual nature. It was then that I realized that he and the others were never my true friends. They were willing to spend several dollars on an alcoholic drink but not spend less money for a glass of tea. I was now able to see them through un-drugged eyes for what they were in relationship to me. I turned and walked out and never returned.

Don't Mind Me. I'm Going To Be Weird For a Few Weeks.

If you are fortunate to have a few important people left in your life who haven't totally abandoned you, i.e. a spouse, parent, or child, and you all live under the same roof . . . it is important that you advise them that you intend to overcome your habit and improve your life and your relationship with them and stop your drinking/using. They need to know that you may very well be displaying mood swings, irritability, and possible physical symptoms. Give them warning.

Once you begin your recovery, you can expect to experience a floodgate of unexplained emotions that come at you like a freight train. You don't know why these feeling come upon you and you don't want to know why. You only want these feelings to go away but you feel unable to do anything about them. You used to drink the reasons away or get high or drugged to the point of not giving a damn and avoiding these reasons and subsequent emotions. You may even consider drinking/using again just to make them go away because that's always worked for you. But Don't!! This is what caused your addiction in the first place. Just let the emotions go away by changing your thoughts and/or doing something different than you were doing when the emotions first started to come upon you.

Others will want to know what's happening while you are experiencing these moods and at a time when you just want them to leave you alone and not ask questions.   Tell them up front that if and when these moods occur, not to take them personally and that they are things that you will be going through to overcome your addiction.   Let them know that the best thing they can do to help you is not try to help you. What you are feeling is a normal reaction to facing the things you have been avoiding all the times you have been drinking, using, or other compulsive behaviors. Any medication that is designed to work on the brain will inhibit your recovery by affecting your brain's ability to recognize the source of your unhappiness and be creative in resolving it.

Politely tell those who may be concerned that it has nothing to do with them and that there's nothing they can do to help you other than to allow you to have these moments and that you need to ride out whatever it is you're feeling.

Let them know that if you happen to slip and fall along the way, the last thing you need to hear from them is their criticizing and you need to have their support to try again. If you do happen to relapse, look at it as a part of your recovery as why it happened and be ready for it if it happens again.

Those with whom you have been living during your compulsive behaviors have created coping skills to deal with your madness and moods over the years. When you begin to remain abstinent, they may not necessarily stop their adopted behaviors that they have relied upon to deal with you.   I have seen many marriages end when an addict or alcoholic becomes clean and sober because others didn't change how they behaved towards the addict when they were drinking/using.   While you may change, the people in your life, most likely, have not. They may continue to criticize, blame, complain, nag, threaten, punish, or bribe or reward you to shame and control you. One of the reasons why others may not change when you do is due to their unwillingness to forgive. They may continue to carry resentment about the past as well as habitual behaviors in dealing with you during the times you were drinking/using. They need time to readjust their thinking and behavior as well.

Addictions affect everyone, not just the addict. Al-Anon is a program for families and loved ones that offer support and teaches new ways to cope and deal with an addictive person. Like A.A., it is free. Another option is to get family counseling. Some alcohol and drug treatment programs offer "family night" once a week while a person is in treatment.

If you don't like yourself, how can you expect others to like you?

Before you can begin to improve and have meaningful relationships with others, you must first have a satisfying relationship with yourself. If you're like most individuals with addictions, you don't think very much of yourself. You may be filled with shame and guilt based on your perception of yourself as a result of what others have said to you and all of the things you have said and done while under the influence or the spell of your non-substance addictive behaviors. Carrying a lot of baggage of past hurts, injustice, both real and imagined, and shame and guilt comes with a price.

Others, even strangers, pick up on your expressions and behaviors that subtly alert them that something is not healthy or "right" with you. They may be friendly towards you but they keep from getting too close. They can sense that you are struggling with something that raises a red flag and tells them not to get any closer than being friendly or a casual acquaintance, if that.

On the flip side of this are those who feel they are just as flawed as you are and they feel comfortable being with you as their friend. Like-minded individuals tend to attract each other. Those with addiction behaviors receive a bit of comfort knowing they are not alone in their lifestyle. Those who drink/drug/or behave in solitude are those who don't want others to know just how much and how often they do what they do. So they do it where no one can see them.

Immediately stop criticizing, blaming, complaining, nagging, punishing, threatening, or making conditional deals with others. Other people in your life have been doing these things to you but that doesn't mean you have to retaliate in like manner. You can choose to stop doing them. What others do is their problem. Don't let their problems become your problems. You have enough of your own to deal with.

There is little doubt that where you were, where you are, and where you will be in life is determined by the choices you make.

Forgive Yourself

Whatever you may have said and done that harmed others, as well as yourself, has been done. It's over. Nothing can be done to change any of it. The shame and guilt that you have can be so intense that you use or drink to avoid facing them. Whatever may have been said and done in the past was the result of choosing the best choice you had at that particular time to satisfy your unhappiness. You knew no other methods at that particular place and time.

You were trying to get one or more of your Basic Needs for happiness met and your choices you made were all you knew to do at that time. Your actions were done as a means of defensiveness to control others when they were trying to control you. You and everyone else in your life have been behaving in disapproving ways. Not only do they not like you, you don't like you. You may be as angry with yourself as you may be with others.

It's not unusual for someone to begin to remember many of the things they said and did in the past once they become sober. Since none of the things you said and did can be taken back, they can only be acknowledged and realize that you just didn't know any other way. Don't allow this to become excess baggage and lead to further shame and guilt. Accept your past sins of omission and commission. Forgive yourself. The more you kick your own behind, the more you destroy what little self-worth you may have. Let it go. Learning new coping skills and internal control will negate the need to resort back to any such harmful behaviors.

In order to forgive yourself, you have to ask for forgiveness from someone higher than yourself. If religious, rely on God. If you aren't religious, know that you are human and we humans are imperfect. Everyone makes mistakes in their life. You are no exception. Ask those whom you may have hurt for forgiveness or share with someone, whom you respect and trust, any of the things you may deeply regret having done in the past.

Telling someone about a past regretful situation often feels like lifting the weight of the world off your shoulders. It also rids you of feeling that you must constantly protect the secrets of your past. Having to stay vigilant to hide past transgressions is very energy consuming and takes a lot of effort to maintain. It drains you of your energy and happiness.

Keep in mind, not everyone may be willing to forgive you and that's okay. At least you offered. It's not important that they forgive you. It's only important that you made an attempt to make things right. If others refuse to forgive you, then who has the problem? Any refusal to forgive you is their choice so accept it and get on with your own life. Ask for forgiveness for your sake, not theirs.

You have an ongoing relationship with your alcohol, drug, or compulsive behavior. They have become your sweetheart and the love of your life in your Quality World image of what is important to you. It has become the way you have chosen to acquire your Basic Needs, albeit only slightly, as well as making your needs even more lacking in fulfillment.

Not only have others been behaving towards you in unwanted ways, you have been doing the same with them. Neither of you are willing to do what you both want each other to do. You dislike them for what they have said and done and you also dislike yourself for what you have been saying and doing to them. They feel the same way.

In order to acquire and maintain abstinence, sobriety, and recovery, you have to forgive yourself.

What has been commonly called "baggage" that people carry about themselves is all the shame, guilt, and anger from the past that they continue to hold onto. So, you screwed up. Welcome to the human race.

Even though you have made poor choices, you aren't alone. All of us have done so . . . some more than others. If you don't know what to do, then how can you do anything? This is where Choice Theory comes into play. Choice Theory is what you can do when you don't know what to do.

How Do I Get There?

You've read several times in this book of my use of the word "control." For months and even years, you have been trying to directly control your emotions and physiology with drugs, alcohol, and other non-substance compulsive behaviors. Drugs and alcohol are highly effective when wanting to mood change and feel physically and emotionally better. They are instant fixes but are only short-lived and a temporary cover-up from what is really bothersome in your life. Occupying your mind with repeated behaviors is an emotional diversion by keeping you from ruminating unwanted thoughts. They also make each day pass quickly before escaping by way of sleeping or passing out.

Other behaviors such as anxiety, depression, and schizophrenia can also be commonly used to get attention and control others. All maladaptive behaviors serve to ease frustration, suppress anger, and/or control others while, at the same time, create some amount of happiness or pleasure.

Forgive Others

Let go of any angry emotions you may have with others whom you feel have wronged you, both real and imagined. Whatever others may have done or said to you was done out of external control by those who were trying to get their power needs met. They didn't know any other way to deal with their unhappiness at the time. They don't realize that the only people they can control in their life is themselves.

When others behave in ways in which you disapprove, the first person who must change is you. The following choices are the only things you can do to change not only yourself, but it will also directly affect others and how they react to you.

Change what you expect of others or how you want them to behave. You aren't going to change them no matter how much they may try to change you. When you stop wanting them to change, you are changing what you are thinking which will change how you feel emotionally and physically. Stop wanting others to live up to your satisfaction. You already know how difficult it is for you to make changes yourself. So what makes you think you can get anyone else to change?

Change how you behave when others don't behave the way you want them to behave. They may use external control to get you to do what they want you to do. Whatever you usually do in your reaction to them not only fails to be effective for you, it lets the offender feel powerful. You take away their power when you stop reacting to their external controls. Changing your behavior will save you from anger, grief, and further harm to the relationship.

If you normally reached for your drug, alcohol, or other compulsive behavior to escape your unhappiness when dealing with others, your past experience with this reaction should tell you that the only thing this behavior did was give you temporary relief and, in many cases, result in hangovers, depression and resolved absolutely nothing.   Why continue to do things that don't work and only make you feel worse?   It's like drinking poison and waiting for the other person to die.

People are totally powerless to control you without you reacting to them. Don't give them permission to attempt to ruin your day.   You always have a choice on how to react to others.

Starting now . . . this very minute . . .and for the rest of your life . . . whenever you feel unhappy or angry. . . **Change what you want and/or change how you behave when you don't get what you want**. Any one, or both of those choices, will have an incredible effect on your life. The more you rely on them, the more they become second nature and you will eventually attain more peace and happiness than you ever thought possible.

Forgiving releases any pain that has been weighing you down for past and present hurts that were inflicted on you as well as those you inflicted on others. It also allows you to choose to never allow any future attempts from others to cause you aggravation and emotional pain.

Be Grateful

Whether you have any religious values or not, the best prayer you can offer to the universe is "Thank you." Right now, you may not be feeling very grateful for very much in your life. If you perceive everything in your life as a meaningless void, then any and all of your choices and anything else that comes to you will look the same . . . meaningless.

For wherever you do or whatever you have, say "Thank You." Even if you can't think of anything to be thankful for, say "Thank You." When you go to sleep tonight and when you wake tomorrow morning, say, "Thank You." Notice anything and everything around you and say, "Thank You." Just for the hell of it, say "THANK YOU!."

Be thankful for all of the bad things that have happened to you. They have given you experience and guidance for future reference. Be thankful for all of your failed relationships for what they gave you when times were good as well as bad. For those whom you feel have hurt you, tell each of them in your mind, "Thank you." They have taught you something about yourself as well as about them. For every adversity there is an equal or greater benefit if you look for it. Say "Thank You." Say "Thank You" for your addiction. If not for your addiction, you would not be where you will be tomorrow from the choices you will be making today and tomorrow. Things are looking better already.

A Simple Relationship Exercise

There are three elements that make up all of our relationships with the important people in our lives.

There is you, the other person, and in between the two of you is the relationship itself. All of the things you say and do to and with another person affect that relationship.

When attempting to repair a damaged relationship, it only makes sense to say and do something that will help the relationship rather than harm it. What can you do for the sake of the relationship with a person you may be experiencing difficulty? Whatever it is, you must want to do it for the sake of the relationship and not for the sake of the other person.

Some examples of things to do for a relationship might be:

> Spending more time at home.
> Doing things you used to do in the past with each other.
> Apologize for past external and distancing behaviors.
> Dinner
> Movies
> Hanging out: listening to music; - discussions on interesting topics
> Spending more time together
> Cease all use of the seven distancing habits:
>
>> Criticizing
>> Blaming
>> Complaining
>> Nagging
>> Punishing
>> Threatening
>> Bribing or rewarding to control

And replacing them with:

>Supporting
>Encouraging
>Listening
>Accepting
>Trusting
>Respecting
>Negotiating Differences

Here's a rhetorical question: Do you think that if you overcame your use of alcohol/drugs/ or other compulsive behaviors, it would improve your relationship with someone important to you?

Others have probably been after you to stop your addictive behavior for some time now. I would venture to say that they used every External Control method in this book and more to get you to do something you didn't want to do. You also felt they were trying to control you, which they were, and you typically resisted anything and everything they wanted or demanded. I get that.

But this time, it's YOUR choice and not theirs. It makes a difference when you make the decision because you want to do it and not because others demand that you do it.

Whatever you choose to do must be done **specifically for the sake of the relationship and not for the other person.** When you focus on the relationship, the other person will indirectly benefit. When you change your behavior, it's amazing how others will react to it.

Stress and boredom are the major reasons why people have difficulty overcoming their addictions. You have been relying on your drug/alcohol or other addictive behavior to deal with stress and boredom, as well as your unhappiness, and drinking/using have become second nature to you.

The fact that you are even thinking about giving up your addictive behavior can be so stressful that you may want to rely on using/drinking before you even begin. The thought that you will be giving up something that you have relied on for years to get by in life can be overwhelming. It's worse than having to say "goodbye" forever to your best friend and lover.

When all you know to do to relieve your stress, anxiety, or boredom is drink/use or other compulsive behavior, this should be a no-brainer: You need to learn new coping skills.

Manage your time. Make lists of what needs to be done and do them without procrastination. Putting off chores or things that need to be done can only add stress to your life. Develop an attitude of "Do It Now!" You'll be surprised how better you will feel when you have taken care of something that you have been putting off and regretting the need to do it.

Take time for yourself to meditate, listen to music, exercise, associate with emotionally healthy friends. Go to meetings. Help others to overcome their addictions. Some would say that's the same thing as the blind leading the blind. But in AA, we have found that by helping others, we are also helping ourselves. We commonly say, "If you want to keep it, you have to give it away."

Find something to do to occupy your time that does not take away from your regular daily responsibilities or infringe upon your relationship with others. Create or return to a hobby or some other interest that keeps your mind off of your urges to drink, use, or do any other compulsive behavior. I find writing to be not only something I enjoy doing, it also reinforces my beliefs and values. I'm giving to others what I have to give and this only adds more of what I have to give rather than deplete it.

Go back to school and get a GED or finish that college education, or start to acquire a degree. Don't let your age get in the way of keeping you from doing what you may always wanted to do. I went back to school when I was forty-eight and got a new career. You are experiencing the results of my choice to do that by reading this book.

Do you recall, in a previous chapter, my story of the time I returned to my old watering hole after a year of abstinence?   While on that same occasion, one of my past so-called friends asked me, "Where the hell have you been?" I explained that I had gone back to school. He asked, "Will you be going for your Master's degree?" I replied, "There's a good chance of it."   He said, (with typical alcohol affected reasoning that an older age is a problem) "You'll be fifty years old if you do that."   My immediate reply was, "Jim. I'm going to be fifty years old whether I get my Master's degree or not." Substance abuse affects the mind in ways that perceptions are more negative and disadvantageous than they are positive or beneficial.

Just think how good you will feel by accomplishing something you've always wanted to do or doing something that makes you happy. Do It Now! Say "yes" to any and all opportunities. Stop making excuses why you can't do this or can't do that. Just do it. Your self-worth and self-esteem will improve immensely. By saying "Yes" to things being asked or opportunities offered, you will find your life improving as well. It's all a part of getting your Power needs met.

For other stress reducing methods utilizing Choice Theory in Action, I highly recommend the series book "A Choice Theory Psychology Guide to Stress," by Brian Lennon.

Dealing With Difficult People

All human beings, regardless of race, religion, or culture, behave from the moment of birth until death. The purpose of any behavior is the choice we make in our efforts to satisfy any one or more of our five basic and genetic needs for **Survival; Love and Belonging**; the **Power** of Acceptance, Appreciation, Respect, Achievement, and Control (Positive or negative); **Freedom** to come and go as we please and make our own decisions; and **Fun** in the form of learning and recreation.

You and I, and everyone else, have developed many behaviors to satisfy these happiness needs from what we have learned from parents, teachers, and from our personal experiences. We also invented some behaviors on our own when all else we knew to meet our happiness wants and needs had failed.

Just like yourself, those with whom you may experience difficulty are only trying to get their Basic Needs met and are likely relying on the need for Power to be satisfied. They do so by using any one or more of the seven distancing habits of External Control to control you. You have reacted in like manner by wanting to get your Power needs satisfied and relied on the same behaviors as they have with you.

Whatever or whoever it is that we want to control will serve to satisfy one or more of our five basic needs. What leads to frustration and unhappiness is trying to control people and things that we cannot control. Relationship conflict is the result of both individuals trying to control each other and to satisfy their Power Needs.

The following is from my Book, "Mentally Ill or Frustrated and Unhappy" vi

If I am having a problem with another person, I don't call "Clamenza" to "take care of it." Nor do I choose to look at other options that I can do to get even or coerce the other person to change.

The key here, when in conflict with others, is "Acceptance." The situation is what it is. Other people are who and what they are so accept that fact. Acceptance does not mean agreeing with them. It means you accept that this is how they

---

vi Rice, Michael, "Mentally Ill or Frustrated and Unhappy?," Pp. 278-279. Madeira Publishing, AZ., 2018

are and what they believe and you are not about to be able to change them. So, accept this fact and save yourself the effort and aggravation.

When it comes to differences of opinion, you may highly disagree with someone but know that no amount of arguing or debate will ever cause them to change their position. So why even bother? How many times have you gotten in a heated discussion with someone and you walked away having transformed their thinking? I would venture to guess you had no success in doing so. This is where Paul McCartney's mother Mary would tell him, "Let It Be" comes into play. It is what it is so move on knowing there's nothing you can do about it. Accept them and their position as it is what it is and it's uncontrollable on your part.

I find it so very amusing that so many people are willing to argue with people they don't even know on Facebook. They resort to name calling and criticizing and all the other External Controlling methods to win an argument and get a complete stranger to believe the way they believe.   How many times have you ever convinced someone whom you know to change their beliefs much less someone you have never met or know anything about?   When someone challenges you on Facebook, you have a choice to think negatively, take it personally, have immediate negative emotions, and choose to argue and fight with them. Or . . . you can use the split second before you react to choose to let them think and believe whatever they want. Why choose to lose your own happiness and contentment and give them the power to do so by your reactions by arguing and using External Control on each other? Why allow someone whose relationship to you is of absolutely no importance whatsoever cause you to choose to get angry and upset? LET IT BE.

You cannot be all things to all people. Don't even try. Those who may continue to have a problem with you during and after your recovery are the only people with the problem. Don't make their problem your problem. You have a choice. You can allow them to be who and what they are . . .they accept you or don't accept you . . .and move on with your life. Or you can choose to get all upset and have a floodgate of emotions that make you feel bad and possibly lead you to return to your old standby of dealing with difficult people . . . drugs or alcohol or other compulsive behaviors. You can choose to waste your time trying to control and change others to get them to like you all for naught. It is what it is. Let it be. The problem is theirs so don't make it yours.

If you have been absorbing the Choice Theory components, you might be thinking to yourself, "Hey, Choice Theory guy! Isn't what you are doing by writing this book essentially telling us what is right for us because it is right for you? You got me. In one sense, the answer is a definite "Yes." However, the purpose behind this book is not to control you. You still have the choice to see its benefits and have a positive effect on your life if you apply it or simply disregard any or all of it and keep on doing what you're doing and continuing to keep on getting what you're getting. I'm only offering you information. What you do with it is your choice. The choice is yours and it is not my place to convince you or coerce you otherwise. (end of book passage).

Getting started is always the hardest part to get clean and sober. Once you see the need, choose to do something about it, and take the first step to change, it gets easier along the way. I can't make you stop drinking, using, or any other compulsive behavior. Neither can anyone else. I can only offer you help and guidance in doing so. I sincerely hope this book will inspire you do take action and take back control of your life filled with happiness and success.

You Can't Do It Alone

This book is not meant to replace the need to get personal counseling or treatment so that you can get clean and sober on your own. You already know by now that you can't do this on your own. If you could do it on your own, you would have stopped a long time ago. There are several addiction treatment agencies available that range in cost from zero to thousands of dollars and everything in between. I don't advocate one on one treatment as I have found it to be lacking in overall effectiveness. Group therapy sessions tend to be the most effective. Why? Because they consist of people just like yourself and you can't B.S. them any more than anyone can B.S. you.

If you are a United States veteran, the Veterans Administration has a free program for you. The Salvation Army has a program. Reference alcohol and drug treatment (or other addiction) programs on the Internet. If you don't have a computer, go to your local library and use any one of those available. Ask those whom you may know who have found sobriety and freedom from addiction where they went to get help. And don't omit A.A. or any other 12-step programs. They're free of cost.

If you aren't financially strapped yet, find a professional agency that specializes in addictions that is affordable. I say this because if you have a financial investment in your recovery, you will be more inclined to want to get something out of the program and treatment more so than if it wasn't costing you anything. Freud supposedly said, "If you want to get better, you have to pay for it."

A.A. groups tend to have a personality all their own based upon the personalities of those who regularly attend the meeting. If you don't feel comfortable or have trouble relating to the members, find another meeting somewhere else until you find one you like and with those whom you can better relate. It works if you work it. So, work it. You're worth it.

6. How A Loved One Can Help

At the risk of sounding cavalier, the answer to the above question is, "You can't." You can only help yourself. The only person whose behavior you can control is your own. If you're like the majority of those who call me seeking help with someone they love or care for, you have tried everything you can think of to get them to stop drinking or using. Your methods may have started out as genuine care and concern for them. After the realization that those methods didn't work, you probably felt frustrated and powerless to do anything to get your loved one to stop drinking or using.

The next steps commonly relied upon is to resort to the seven deadly habits of relationship distancing behaviors of criticizing, blaming, complaining, nagging, threatening, punishing, or even bribing them to get them to behave the way you want them to behave.   Your intentions, although honorable, only led to the person you care about to drink or use even more in order to avoid   having to deal with your methods and having to facing their own shame and guilt.

Your loved one is addicted to drugs or alcohol and you have become addicted to them by way of frustration and your failure to get them to do what you want them to do. They are consuming most of your thoughts and behaviors to get them to change.   You may have trouble sleeping or concentrating on your own needs. You worry and feel anxious.   You wrack your brain thinking of other things you might do to get them to stop. You have run out of creative ideas other than to call a professional who will tell you that there is nothing you can do other than conduct a conventional intervention that will consist of more external controlling behaviors that fail more than they succeed.

Both of you need to turn your backs on one another and learn something that will have a positive effect on your happiness and wellbeing and then get back together at a later time utilizing your newfound knowledge and awareness.

First: Stop using the seven deadly habits of relationship destroying behaviors.   You will both feel better once you stop doing them.

Second: Learn and understand the nature of addiction as outlined in this book. Addiction is not a character disorder but a means of surviving to avoid withdrawal symptoms and dealing with unpleasant emotions and situations in their life. It is often the result of a biochemical condition created after longtime usage and cellular adaptation.

Third: Start doing things for yourself rather than worrying, losing sleep, feeling anxious, and consuming your daily thoughts about the person with whom you are concerned. See to your own needs instead of giving them up for the sake of someone else.

Fourth: I highly recommend going to Al-anon meetings. Al anon is an organization of individuals who are in the same situation as yourself. They are in love with or care for someone close to them who has a substance abuse problem. The 12 steps of Al anon are practically word for word the same 12 steps as Alcoholic Anonymous. You will hear stories from regular members of how these steps improved their life and eased their frustration dealing and living with someone who is addicted. And it's free. There are also CODA meetings (codependents anonymous). You may also opt to seek one on one counseling; however, you will probably find better results from such groups as Al anon.

Looking at the above suggestions, you will note that they are designed to deal with you and your unhappiness and not the other person. You can only control your own behavior. Attempting to control the behavior of someone else will always result in disappointment, frustration, and anger. You help others best by being better, yourself.

Once you begin to focus on your own wants and needs, don't be surprised if your loved one decides to take measures to deal with their own issues. This would be the result of your cessation of criticizing and nagging them about their addiction and for them to save face by making the decision theirs and not yours. If this, indeed, does happen, it won't happen overnight. Showing that you no longer concern yourself with their behavior can lead to the possibility that they may think you don't care anymore and that they may lose you.

This possibility leads me to admit that there is one external controlling behavior that you may utilize when all else has failed: Threatening to leave. If this method is relied upon, be prepared to follow through with the threat and leave. If not, they will only hear your threat as empty rhetoric. Unfortunately, there are situations where you must divorce yourself from those who are close to you for the sake of your own happiness and health. It is often those who are closest to us who are the most toxic to our own life. It is okay to divorce yourself from toxic people even if they are family. You deserve a life of happiness without allowing those close to you to prevent it.

When all you have done for yourself has failed to satisfy your own happiness and wellbeing, you have the choice of continuing to live a life of misery and poor emotional and physical health or distancing yourself from the person and the problem.

7. Epilogue

I have seen and helped many extremely compulsive drinkers and users find their way back to sobriety and free from their drugs. I can't take credit for it because it is they and their support group that got them there. All I can do is give you information to help guide you along the way to the happiness and serenity of being clean and sober. You can't do it alone and if you are like most of us, you have tried to do it alone several times. It's so very important to acknowledge that the cessation of your alcohol or drug, alone, will not afford you the happiness and peace of mind you wish to achieve. Abstinence is one thing. Recovery is yet another. You will need to acquire both abstinence and recovery.

Recovery is the process of learning many of the coping and life skills needed to deal with your past hurts and trauma by not revisiting them and learning how to move forward using healthy, connecting, relationship skills. Recovery is an ongoing learning process that will involve several years of your future experiences with your newfound knowledge of connecting with others. With each new learned lesson, you will smile and even be grateful for all of your past addiction. If not for your addiction, you cannot fully appreciate just how successful you are and how far you have come since getting clean and sober. We can't appreciate light if there is no darkness.

You deserve to be happy. We all do. Drinking, using, and other compulsive behaviors are not, will not, and never will be the way to happiness and peace of mind. In fact, those are the behaviors that destroy happiness and peace of mind. Life is short enough without living it in misery and unhappiness. True happiness is the result of meaningful relationships with at least one person .. .. preferably more. Peace of mind is the result of being responsible, having a source of adequate income, being appreciated and respected, taking care of obligations, getting along with others, learning and having fun while being free of encumbrances in order to make healthy choices.

Further Reading

Books by Dr. Glasser

- Choice Theory in the Classroom
- Choice Theory: A New Psychology For Personal Freedom
- Counseling With Choice Theory: The New Reality Therapy
- Eight Lessons For A Happier Marriage
- Every Student Can Succeed
- Fibromyalgia: Hope From A Completely New Perspective
- For Parents and Teenagers: Dissolving the Barriers Between Them
- Getting Together and Staying Together
- Reality Therapy: A New Approach to Psychiatry
- Schools Without Failure
- Take Charge of Your Life
- The Choice Theory Manager
- The Control Theory Manager
- The Language of Choice Theory
- The Quality School
- The Quality School Teacher
- Warning: Psychiatry Can Be Hazardous To Your Mental Health
- What Is This Thing Called Love

These books are available in bookshops and libraries but may be obtained from wglasserbooks.com

Books on Psych Meds: Their Addiction and Withdrawal

- Your Drug May Be Your Problem, How and Why to Stop Taking Psychiatric Medications, Peter R. Breggin M.D.
- Toxic Psychiatry, Peter R. Breggin M.D.
- Medication Madness, Peter R. Breggin M.D.
- Pharmageddon, David Healy
- Bad Pharma: How drug companies mislead doctors and harm patients, Ben Goldacre
- Deadly Medicines and Organized Crime: How Bi Pharma Has Corrupted Healthcare, Peter Gøtzsche.
- Beyond Prozac: Healing Mental Distress, Dr. Terry Lynch

Other Books by Michael Rice

A Choice Theory Approach to Drug and Alcohol Abuse
    ISBN: 1449501079
    For addicts/alcoholics, therapists/counselors, and anyone who lives with or loves an addicted person.

Til Death Do Us Part, or 'Til You Piss Me Off, Whichever Comes First
    ISBN: 1449503160
    Why marriages and relationships fail and how to put them back together.

Happiness is Just a Bowl of Choices

ISBN: 1449500897

Why people do the things they do which destroy what they want the most in life: Happiness. Learn ways to find and keep it.

Choice Theory with Addicted Populations

ISBN: 146094979X

A Diverse Approach for the Treatment of Addictions. This book contains techniques, directives, ideas, and explanations for those who may be addicted to prescription meds, street drugs or alcohol.

Leave Me Alone!

ISBN: 1497531861

Direct, blunt, and to the point designed for the reader to see the reality and truth of addiction. Directions and concepts are passed along to the reader to assist them on the road to a drug/alcohol-free life and new-found happiness.

Grow Old And Be Happy: A Work in Progress
ISBN: 1532927509
Mike takes an honest, sometimes humorous look at the aging process, grief and mortality from a Choice Theory point of view.

Mentally Ill: or Frustrated and Unhappy?
ISBN: 1983849936
What do you do when you don't know what to do? What do you do after all your attempts to resolve your unhappiness have failed? Feeling powerless to resolve an unhappy situation can lead to physical illnesses and social and psychological problems.

The Choice Theory in Action Series Titles

A Choice Theory Psychology Guide to Addictions: Ways to Overcome Substance Dependence and Other Compulsive Behaviors - Michael Rice

A Choice Theory Psychology Guide to Anger Management: How to Manage Rage in Your Life - Brian Lennon

A Choice Theory Psychology Guide to Depression: Lift Your Mood - Robert E. Wubbolding, Ph.D.

A Choice Theory Psychology Guide to Happiness: How to Make Yourself Happy - Carleen Glasser

A Choice Theory Psychology Guide to Parenting: The Art of Raising Great Children - Nancy S. Buck Ph.D.

A Choice Theory Psychology Guide to Relationships - Kim Olver

A Choice Theory Psychology Guide to Stress: Ways of Managing Stress in Your Life - Brian Lennon

The Choice Theory in Action Series is available from Amazon as e-books or paperbacks and may be obtained through bookshops including wglasserbooks.com

William Glasser International

The body that Dr. Glasser approved to continue teaching and developing his ideas is William Glasser International.

This organisation helps coordinate the work of many member organisations around the world.

WGI recently introduced a six-hour workshop entitled, "Taking Charge of Your Life". This is intended for the general public and provides a good foundation in Choice Theory psychology.

If you are interested in further training in Choice Theory psychology or any of its applications, you are recommended to contact WGI or your nearest member organisation of WGI.

www.wglasserinternational.org